Copyright © 2024 by D. Elizabeth Erasmus.
Copyright Number: 1214234
All rights reserved.
No part of this publication may be reproduced,
distributed, or transmitted in any form or by any means,
including photocopying, recording,
or other electronic
or mechanical methods,
without the prior written permission
of the publisher, except in the case of brief quotations
embodied in critical reviews and certain other
non-commercial uses permitted by copyright law.
For permission requests, write to the Author,
addressed "Attention: Permissions Coordinator,"
at the address below.
P.O. Box 194
Busby,
Alberta
T0G 0H0
Canada

Sammy Goes To The Farm

Written by:
Elizabeth Erasmus

Copyright: 1214234

Illustrator: Minahal Aziz

Meet Sammy
our beloved Labrador.

Find hidden objects on each page
Sammy, Ball, Bee and Dog Bone.

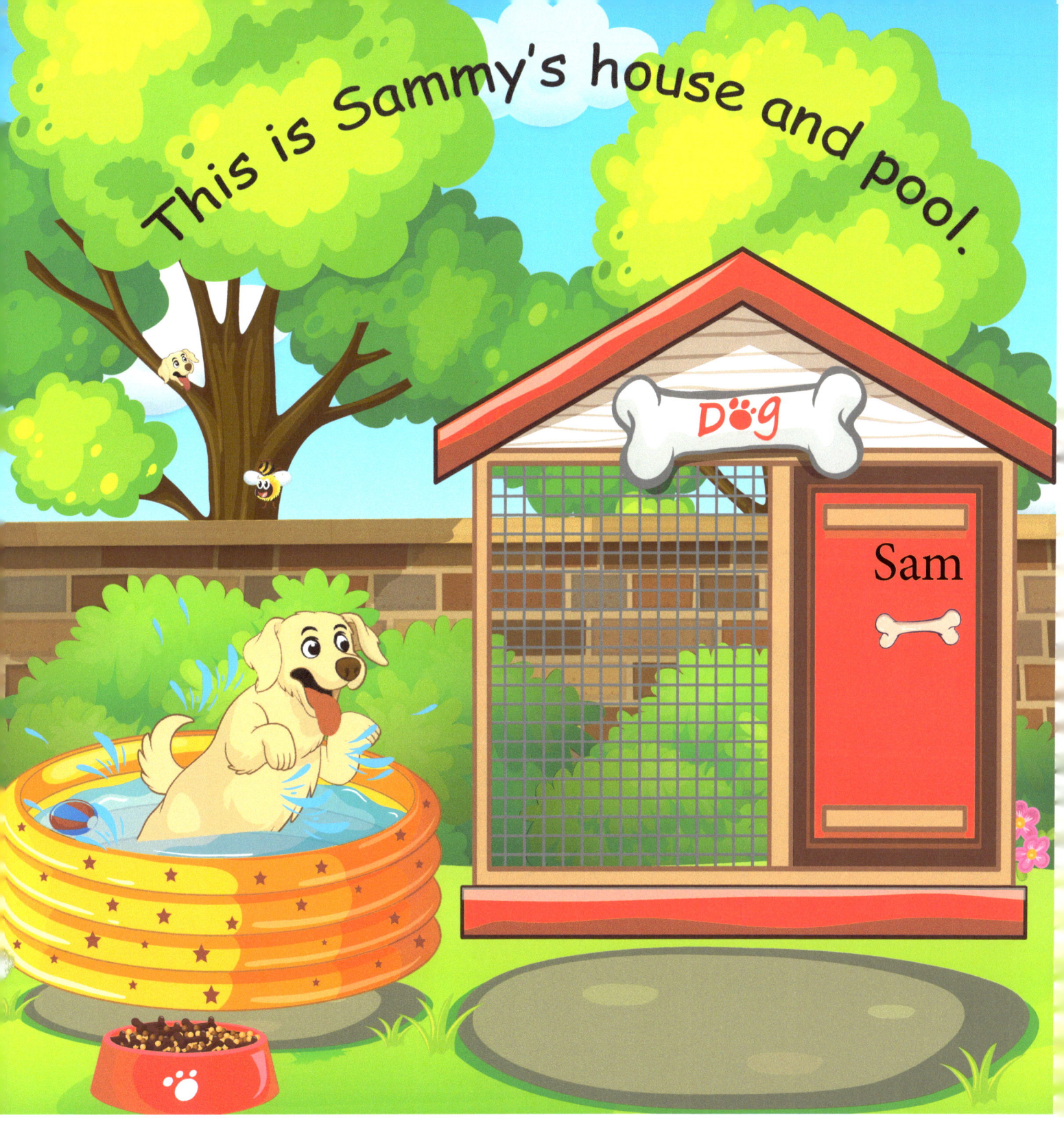

Today is special because Bella, Jack, Sammy, Mom, and Dad are going to the farm. Jack and Bella are packing their clothes for the trip. They can not wait to have fun and explore the farm with Sammy!

Mom and Dad are loading
everything into the car,
making sure that
it will all fit.

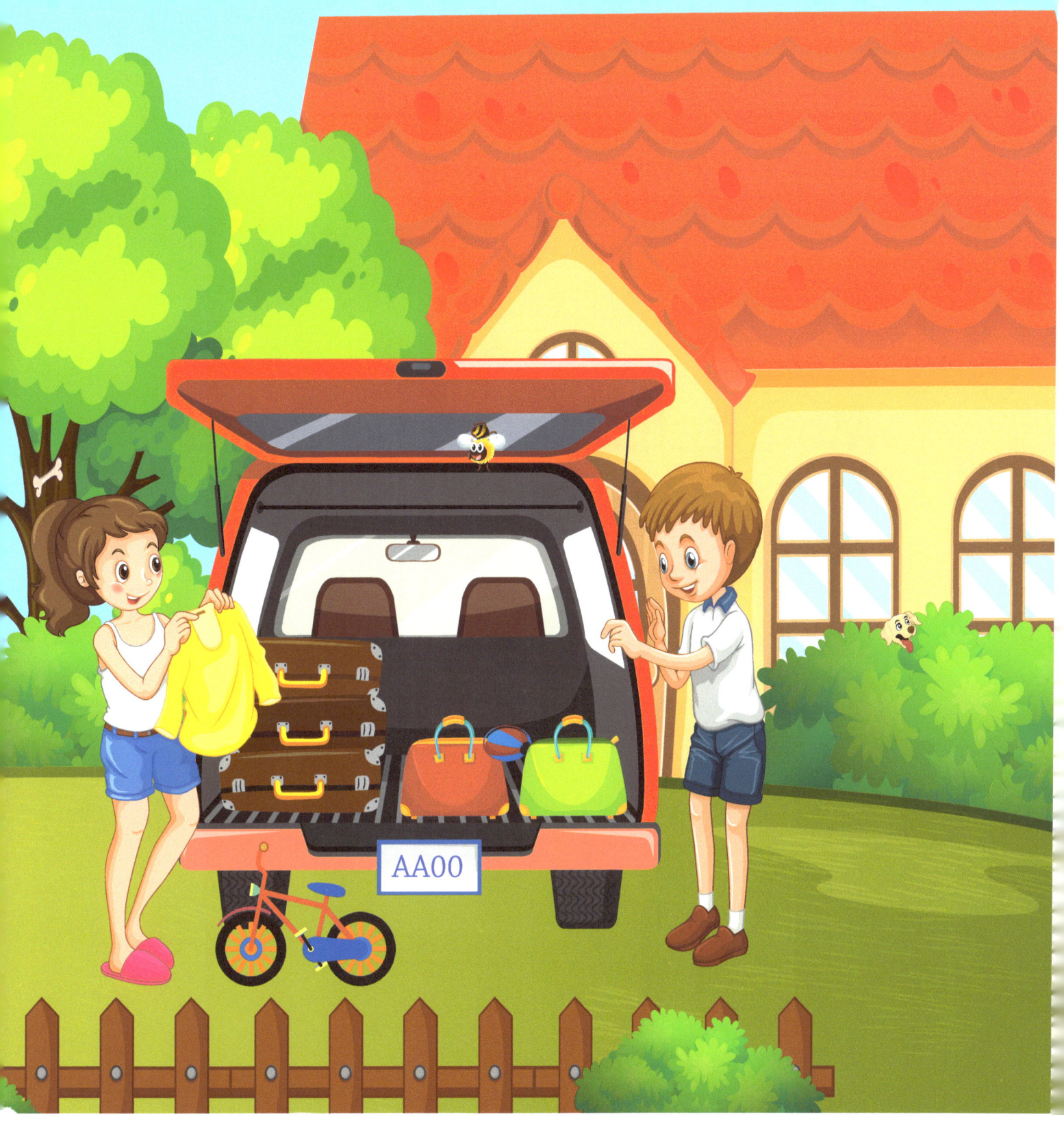

Mom tells Jack and Bella,
"Safety first!
Put on your seat belts.
We are ready to go."

Sammy, Jack, and Bella stop for a rest break at a roadside park.
They enjoy playing on the swings, slides, and climbers.

After playing fetch with Sammy, Jack and Bella are having a picnic with Mom and Dad.

After the long drive, Grandma and Grandpa are happy to see the family. They are waiting in front of the house, ready to greet everyone with warm smiles and hugs.

Sammy and his dog friend Rover
from the farm are happy to see
each other again. They wag their
tails and run to greet
each other.

Peanut the barn cat, along with her two kittens, came to greet Sammy and Rover with a friendly "meow."

Sammy and Rover greet
Daisy, the milk cow,
with a bark, and Daisy
responds with a "moo."

Sammy was amazed to see Gus the donkey, as he had never met a donkey before.
Gus greeted everyone with a "hee-haw!"

Sammy and Rover are having fun swimming in the pond with the ducks and geese. Sam is like a fish in water because he has webbed toes.

Sammy and Rover are taking a break after running and swimming with the ducks and geese.

After a short break
Sammy ran to greet
Mr. Skunk and got sprayed
with skunk spray.
Grandma said
"Sammy, you are a stinky dog,
you need a bath."

Sammy is having a great time taking a bubble bath to wash off the stinky skunk spray.

Mommy and her two little piglets are excited to see everyone; they greet with a happy "squeal."

Sammy peeks through the hole in the fence while Bella and Jack gather eggs from the chicken coop.

After a busy day on the farm, Sammy sleeps on the floor while Mom reads a bedtime story to Jack and Bella.

Today is the final day on the farm. The family is enjoying breakfast together before Grandpa, Dad, and Jack head out to fish in the pond on the farm.

Dad, Grandpa, and
Jack are
fishing at the pond.
Sammy and Rover can
not wait to swim.

Jack, Bella, Sammy, Mom, and Dad are ready to leave. Everyone is buckled in. Bella and Jack shout out the window, "Bye-bye Grandma and Grandpa!"

Back home, Sammy falls asleep quickly after a very busy few days on the farm.

Trace the maze with
your finger to find
where Sammy is hiding.
Can you find him?

Use your finger to trace the path through the maze and find Sammy.

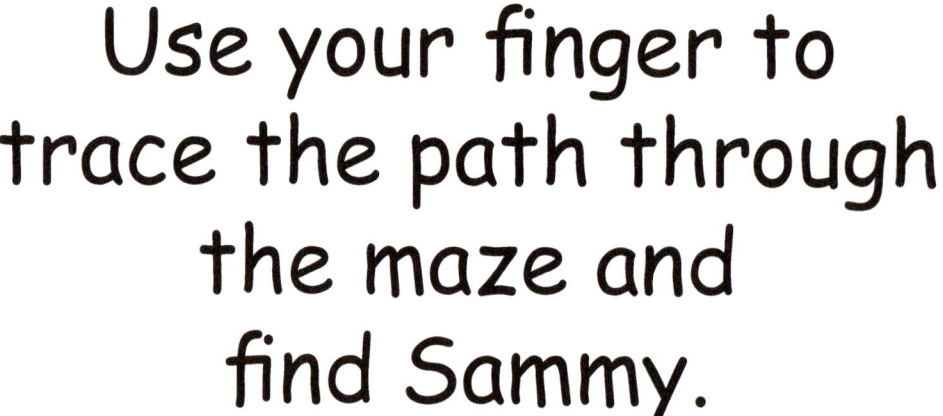

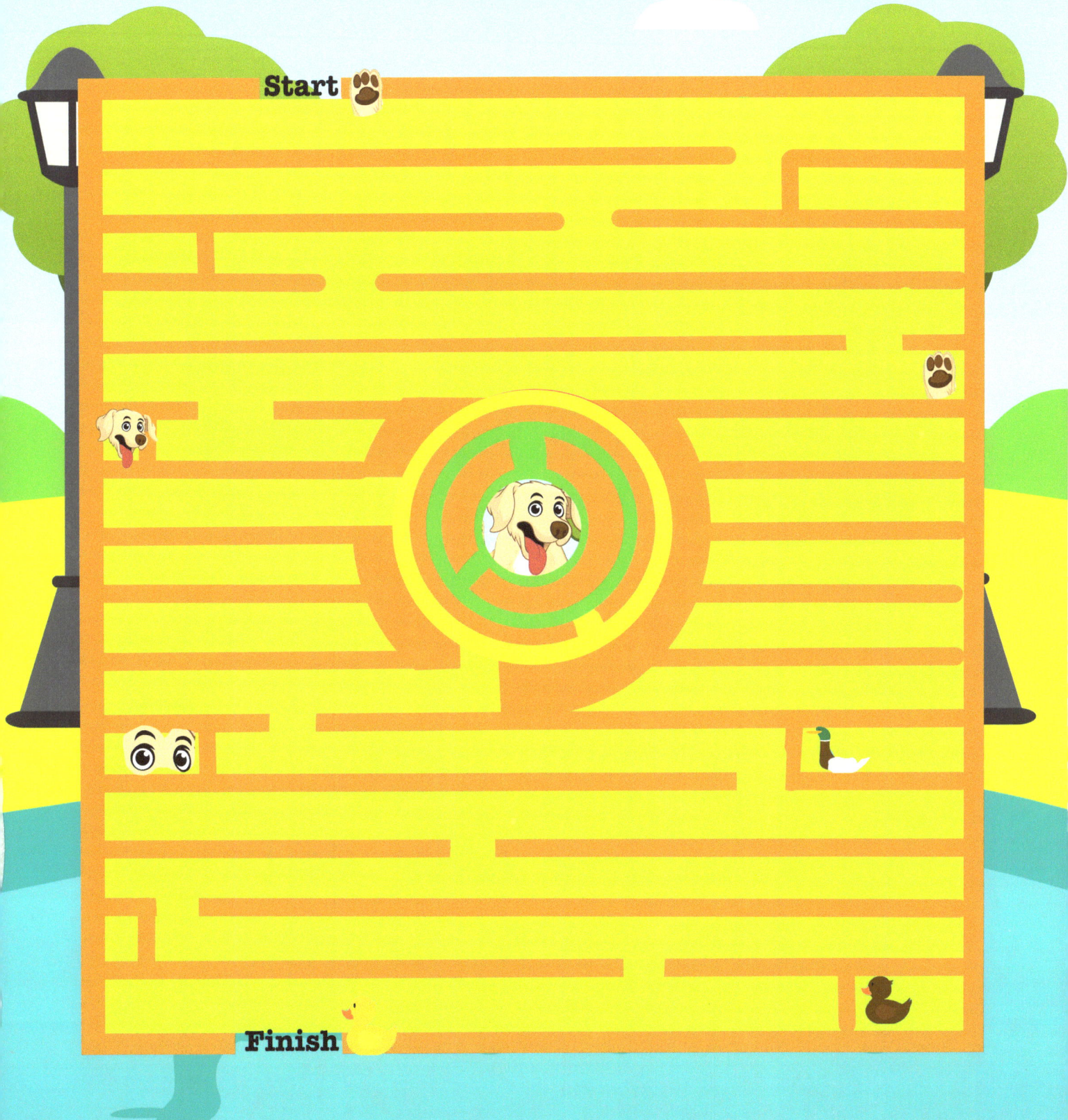

Learning Words

pond   name   farm   breakfast
are   who   meet   around
skunk   fishing   sprayed
water   this   run   fun   don't
says   donkey   butterflies
chase   tree   chicken   rover   bees
is   with   geese
with   dog   cow   cat
best   barn   skunk

Bella is taking Sammy for a walk in the park on a beautiful sunny day.

More Books

Sam's Pawsome Life

Sammy Goes To The Farm

Adventures With Mason and Paisley

Sophia and Calvin's Great Escape:
Desert Sands and Czech Lands

The Secret Life Of Henry the Grasshopper